Montana

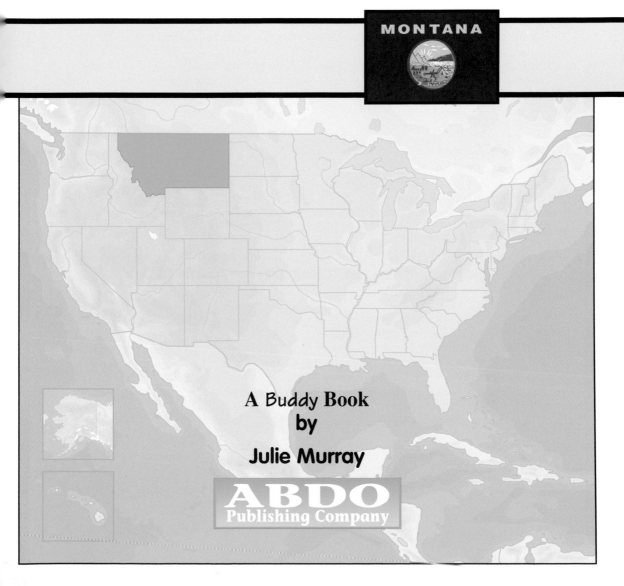

A Buddy Book
by
Julie Murray

ABDO
Publishing Company

VISIT US AT

www.abdopub.com

Published by ABDO Publishing Company, 4940 Viking Drive, Edina, Minnesota 55435.

Copyright © 2006 by Abdo Consulting Group, Inc. International copyrights reserved in all countries. No part of this book may be reproduced in any form without written permission from the publisher. Buddy Books™ is a trademark and logo of ABDO Publishing Company.

Printed in the United States.

Edited by: Sarah Tieck
Contributing Editor: Michael P. Goecke
Graphic Design: Deb Coldiron, Maria Hosley
Image Research: Sarah Tieck
Photographs: Clipart.com, Creatas, Getty Images, Library of Congress, One Mile Up, PhotoDisc, Photos.com

Library of Congress Cataloging-in-Publication Data

Murray, Julie, 1969-
    Montana / Julie Murray.
        p. cm. — (The United States)
    Includes index.
        Contents: A snapshot of Montana — Where is Montana? — All about Montana — Cities and the capital — Famous citizens — The Battle of Little Bighorn — Montana's wildlife — Glacier National Park — A history of Montana.
    ISBN 1-59197-685-5
        1. Montana—Juvenile literature. I. Title.

F731.3.M87 2006
978.6—dc22

                                              2005045734

Table Of Contents

A Snapshot Of Montana 4

Where Is Montana? 7

Fun Facts 12

Cities And The Capital 14

Famous Citizens 16

The Battle Of Little Bighorn 18

Montana's Wildlife 22

Glacier National Park 24

A History Of Montana 28

A State Map 30

Important Words 31

Web Sites 31

Index 32

A Snapshot Of Montana

When people think of Montana, they think of mountains. The Rocky Mountains run through the western part of this state. The Rocky Mountains are a major network of mountains that stretch 3,000 miles (4,828 km) from Alaska to New Mexico. Even the state's name comes from a Spanish word meaning "mountainous."

The Mission Mountains are some of the mountains in Montana.

There are 50 states in the United States. Every state is different. Every state has an official nickname. Montana is sometimes called the "Treasure State." This refers to the importance of mining in Montana. Both gold and silver have been found there.

Mining is an important industry in Montana.

Montana became the 41st state on November 8, 1889. Today, it is the fourth-largest state in the United States. Montana has 147,047 square miles (380,850 sq km). It is home to 902,195 people.

Where Is Montana?

There are four parts of the United States. Each part is called a region. Each region is in a different area of the country. The United States Census Bureau says the four regions are the Northeast, the South, the Midwest, and the West.

Four Regions of the United States of America

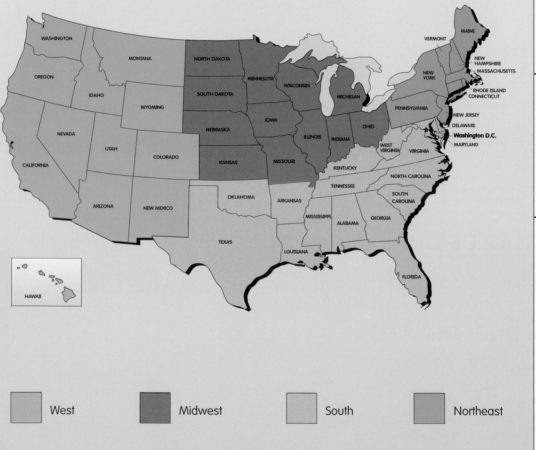

West	Midwest	South	Northeast

Montana is located in the West region of the United States. Montana has four seasons. The seasons are spring, summer, fall, and winter. Montana's weather is mild and changes quickly.

Spring in Montana.

Montana shares its borders with four other states and the country of Canada. North Dakota and South Dakota are neighbors to the east. Wyoming is to the south. Idaho lies to the west. Canada is to the north.

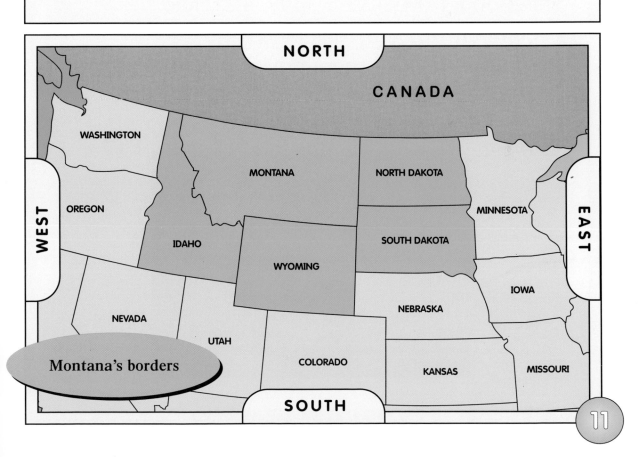

Montana's borders

Montana

State abbreviation: MT

State nickname: Treasure State

State capital: Helena

State motto: *Oro y plata* (Spanish for "Gold and Silver")

Statehood: November 8, 1889, 41st state

Population: 902,195, ranks 44th

Land area: 147,047 square miles (380,850 sq km), ranks fourth

State flag:
Adopted in 1905

State tree: Ponderosa pine

State song: "Montana"

State government: Three branches: legislative, executive, and judicial

Average July temperature: 68°F (20°C)

Average January temperature: 18°F (-8°C)

State flower: Bitterroot

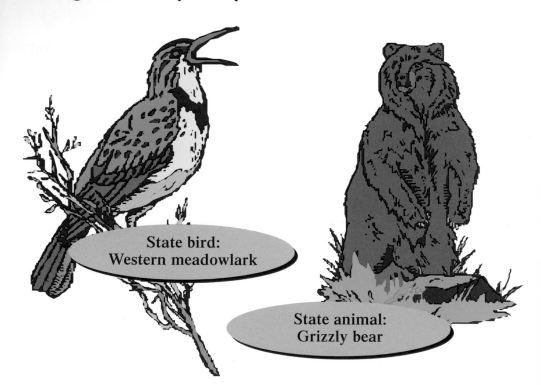

State bird: Western meadowlark

State animal: Grizzly bear

Cities And The Capital

Billings is the largest city in Montana. It is located in the south central part of the state along the Yellowstone River. Billings was named after Frederick Billings, a former president of the Northern Pacific Railroad. During the late 1800s, the first railroads were built through Billings.

Helena became Montana's state capital in 1875. It is located in the west central part of the state. Today, Last Chance Gulch is one of Helena's main streets. Miners found gold in Last Chance Gulch in 1864.

The Capitol is in Helena.

Famous Citizens

Jeannette Rankin (1880–1973)

Jeannette Rankin was born near Missoula in 1880. She was the first woman elected to the United States House of Representatives. She represented Montana in Congress from 1917 to 1919, and again from 1941 to 1943. She voted against the United States entering both World War I and World War II.

Jeannette Rankin

Famous Citizens

Jack Horner (1946–)

Jack Horner was born in Shelby in 1946. He is a **paleontologist** who has found many dinosaur fossils and eggs. His discoveries showed that dinosaurs may have cared for their young. Horner served as a technical adviser for the *Jurassic Park* movies.

Jack Horner

The Battle Of Little Bighorn

The Battle of Little Bighorn was fought in Montana in 1876. It was a famous battle between the United States and the Native Americans. Today, it is sometimes called "Custer's Last Stand."

The battle took place along the Little Bighorn River. Lieutenant Colonel George Custer led about 650 United States soldiers into battle. It started when Custer and his men attacked a group of Sioux and Northern Cheyenne. The Native Americans were ready for this attack. They had about 2,000 warriors ready to fight.

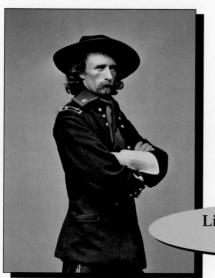

Lieutenant Colonel
George Custer

Sitting Bull and Crazy Horse led the Sioux and Cheyenne to victory. Custer and more than 200 of his soldiers were killed in the Battle of Little Bighorn.

Today, visitors can see where this famous battle took place. It is known as the Little Bighorn Battlefield National Monument.

Sitting Bull

This is what the Little Bighorn Battlefield looks like today.

Montana's Wildlife

Montana is home to a variety of animals. There are bighorn sheep, black bears, grizzly bears, eagles, elk, mountain lions, moose, and pronghorn antelopes.

A grizzly bear with cubs (below) and an eagle (right).

Bison and prairie dogs used to live on Montana's prairie land. Today, there are areas set aside to protect bison and prairie dogs. Hunters killed most of Montana's bison for their meat and hides. Farmers killed prairie dogs because they ruined the farmers' crops.

Today, bison live in protected areas.

Glacier National Park

Glacier National Park is the most visited place in Montana. Glacier National Park is located in the northwestern part of the state. The park also runs into part of Canada.

Some parts of Glacier's mountains
have snow all year long.

Glacier National Park was established in 1910. It has more than 1 million acres (404,686 ha) of wilderness. The park gets its name from the 50 glaciers that are found in the park.

You can see high-peaked mountains, clear blue lakes, wildflowers, and animals at Glacier National Park. Activities at the park include, hiking, biking, camping, canoeing, and fishing.

There are many lakes in Glacier National Park.

Montana

1803: President Thomas Jefferson arranges for the United States to buy Montana as part of the Louisiana Purchase.

1805: Meriwether Lewis and William Clark begin to explore Montana.

1862: Gold is discovered in Montana.

Meriwether Lewis

1876: Native Americans defeat the United States Army at the Battle of Little Bighorn.

1883: The Northern Pacific Railroad is completed through Montana.

1889: Montana becomes the 41st state on November 8.

1910: Glacier National Park is established.

1951: Oil boom begins in eastern Montana.

1972: Montana approves a new constitution.

1989: Montana celebrates its centennial.

2000: Wildfires roar through the state. Nearly 1 million acres (404,686 ha) of land burn.

2005: Events throughout Montana honor the 200th anniversary of Lewis and Clark's exploration of the state.

William Clark

Cities In Montana

Shelby

Great Falls

Glendive

Missoula

★ Helena

Butte

Billings

Important Words

capital a city where government leaders meet.

centennial 100-year anniversary.

Louisiana Purchase a deal where the United States bought land from France. Part of this land later became Montana.

miner a person who digs for minerals or precious metals such as gold.

nickname a name that describes something special about a person or a place.

paleontologist a person who studies fossils of prehistoric life.

World War I the first war between many countries that happened from 1914 to 1918.

World War II the second war between many countries that happened from 1939 to 1945.

Web Sites

To learn more about Montana, visit ABDO Publishing Company on the World Wide Web. Web site links about Montana are featured on our Book Links page. These links are routinely monitored and updated to provide the most current information available.

www.abdopub.com

Index

Alaska.................................**4**

Billings **14, 30**

Billings, Frederick....................**14**

Canada **11, 24**

Clark, William **28, 29**

Crazy Horse **20**

Custer, George **18, 19, 20**

Glacier National
      Park **24, 25, 26, 27, 29**

Helena **12, 15, 30**

Horner, Jack **17**

Idaho...**11**

Jefferson, Thomas.......................**28**

Last Chance Gulch **15**

Lewis, Meriwether................**28, 29**

Little Bighorn, Battle of **18,
      19, 20, 21, 28**

Little Bighorn Battlefield National
      Monument **20, 21**

Little Bighorn River **19**

Midwest **7, 8**

Missoula.............................**16, 30**

New Mexico **4**

North Dakota.................................**11**

Northeast.................................**7, 8**

Northern Cheyenne.......................**19**

Northern Pacific Railroad.......**14, 28**

Rankin, Jeannette **16**

Rocky Mountains **4**

Shelby **17, 30**

Sioux **19**

Sitting Bull **20**

South................................**7, 8**

South Dakota.................................**11**

United States Army **28**

United States Census Bureau **7**

United States House of
      Representatives.......................**16**

West **7, 8, 9**

Wyoming **11**

Yellowstone River **14**